Grand Canyon National Park

Attractions & Sights to See

Billy Grinslott & Kinsey Marie Books

ISBN - 9781960612946

Grand Canyon National Park is bigger than the entire state of Rhode Island. It is 1,904 square miles in size and 1 mile deep. The South Rim is the most popular place to visit at Grand Canyon National Park. The South Rim is located in northern Arizona. The south rim offers many things to do and see. Many trails can be accessed from the South rim.

Bright Angel Trail is considered the most popular hiking trail in the park. It is fairly easy to walk down. This can be a blessing or a curse. You will enjoy wide views of the inner canyon and distant formations. The return hike back up and out of the canyon is far more difficult and requires much more effort. It will take you to some tunnels and resting places. The total length is 12 miles roundtrip, but you can turn around at any point.

Cape Royal Trail is one of two spots with views of the Colorado River from the North Rim. From the southeast end of the parking lot, a .08-mile path leads to several spectacular viewpoints. There is a picnic area on the West side of the parking lot. The dramatic rock formations and view make this a popular spot for viewing at sunset.

Yaki Point is the only viewpoint on Desert View Drive that is not accessible with your vehicle. It can be reached using the free Kaibab Rim Route shuttle bus. from the Grand Canyon Visitor Center. Here the view of the canyon opens to the east, with spectacular views of the canyon. A popular spot for sunset and sunrise, the lack of private vehicles provides a little bit more solitude than other canyon areas.

The Colorado River offers a lot for activities. River rafting and kayaking to name a couple. The Colorado River is nearly 1500 miles long. It runs from the Rocky Mountains to the ocean in Mexico. About 277 miles of the Colorado river runs through the Grand Canyon area. The Colorado river is one of the main attractions for the Grand Canyon. Millions of people visit it every year.

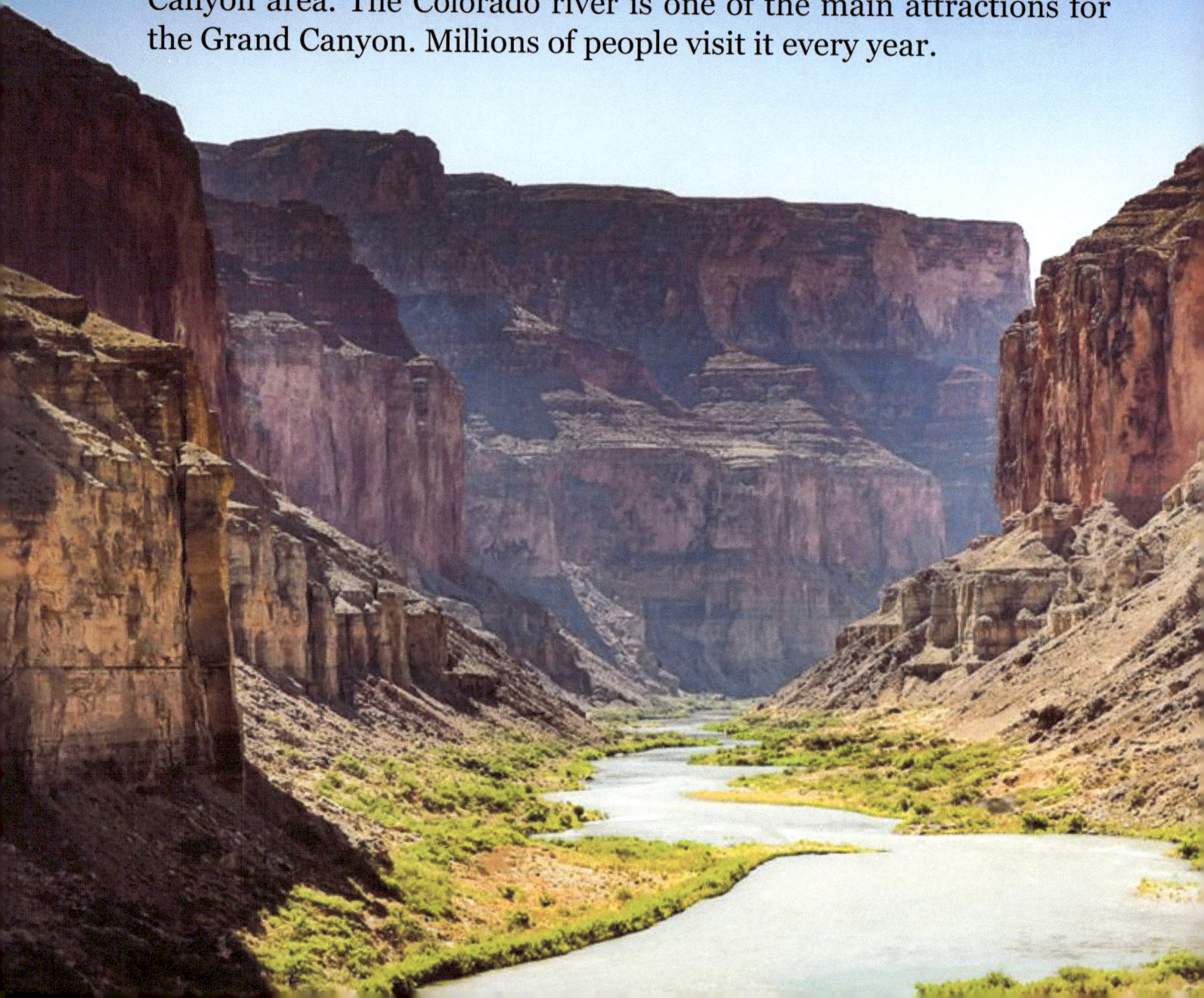

The North Kaibab Trail is the least visited and it is the most difficult of the major inner canyon trails at Grand Canyon. Beginning 1,000 feet higher than South Rim trails, hikers can view the expansive Bright Angel Canyon. The North Kaibab Trail is the only trail on the North Rim that goes to the Colorado River. The way down is better than the hike back to the top. There are several shorter hikes you can take with awesome views of the Grand Canyon.

Point Imperial is the most northern sightseeing spot in the Grand Canyon national park. Visitors have views of the eastern end of the Grand Canyon its walls of Marble. Red and black rock formations and cliff sides. The view has a great contrast of different colors. Imperial is off the main road Rt. 67 into the park. It offers a panorama view of the northeast side of the Grand Canyon and the cliffs and plateaus.

Navajo Point is located just a few minutes west of Desert View on Desert View Drive. Navajo Point offers a great view of the Desert View Watchtower, as well as panoramic views to the west and a view of the Colorado River at the bottom of the canyon. With a dramatic view to the west, and accessible by car, Navajo Point is a popular spot for sunset. Navajo Point is the highest overlook point at 7500 feet on the South Rim drive.

Yavapai Point provides some of the best views along the South Rim of the Grand Canyon, including part of the Colorado River. Yavapai Point has excellent views but there is limited parking at the trailhead. Head out on this 1.7-mile out-and-back trail, generally considered an easy route. You can also visit the Yavapai Museum It has a large picture window with canyon views. Lots of exhibits and an amphitheater.

Maricopa Point is a short walk from the parking area and rewards viewers with vast open views of the Grand Canyon. The 180-degree view has no significant obstructions down to the bottom of the canyon's depths. Sharp eyes will spot the first tiny view of the Colorado River. Maricopa Point is named for the Maricopa Indians who lived in south-central Arizona. Maricopa Point is located on Hermit Road west of Grand Canyon Village. It is a 4-mile hike roundtrip, generally considered a moderately challenging route.

The Abyss has impressive canyon views that are rivaled by the sheer vertical drop of 3,000 feet. This shows how gravity can affect the shape of the canyon walls. At the Abyss, no fault line is present, meaning very little water runs into the canyon because it mostly drains to the south away from the rim. Instead, it shows what gravity can do to the canyon walls as large fallen boulders rest at the bottom. The Abyss is located on Hermit Road west of Grand Canyon Village.

Lookout Studio creates opportunities for visitors to safely view and photograph the natural beauty of Grand Canyon from its edge. Made of local limestone, it's a multi-level stone building that sits on the edge of Grand Canyon. It is a souvenir shop and viewpoint, with several terraces that allow visitors to a view the canyon from safe spots. Lookout Studio is located on the South Rim Trail

Trail view Overlook. This viewpoint is the first stop on the Hermit Trail. It offers stunning views of the canyon. It is an easy walk from the parking area to the overlook. From this overlook, you can walk downhill along the Canyon. A dirt trail with steps descends into the canyon. There is a moderate one-way trail to Trail view Overlook. A short walk down the stairs from the shuttle stop is the best location for views of the switchbacks. From this viewpoint, you can see down, 3000 feet.

The road to Point Sublime Road offers awesome views into the Grand Canyon. Along the North Rim is Sublime Road, a rough and lonely 18-mile road that leads the sublime point. Point Sublime sticks out into the Grand Canyon, offering the few visitors willing and able to make the trip there a magnificent panorama view of the great Grand Canyon.

little Colorado river overlook. The most popular viewpoint on the rim is the little Colorado river gorge overlook on state route 64 or Desert View Drive between mile markers 285 and 286. You will see a deep canyon with steep cliffs carved out by the Little Colorado River. This site allows you to take pictures and has miraculous views.

Indian garden is now officially called Havasupai gardens. Havasupai Gardens is located on the Bright Angel Trail approximately halfway between the South Rim and the Colorado River. Experience this 8.9-mile out-and-back trail, generally considered a challenging route. Havasupai Gardens is along the Bright Angel Trail and is a frequent stop for day hikers and backpackers exploring the backcountry of Grand Canyon. There are plenty of spots to camp along this trail.

The South Kaibab Trail is a well-maintained dirt trail offering wonderful expansive views of the canyon. This is a great trail for short trips into the canyon of half a day or less. The openness of this trail lends itself to extreme heat during the summer months and little protection from passing storms. The total length is 6 miles roundtrip, but you can turn around at any point. The North Kaibab Trail is the least visited and most difficult of the major inner canyon trails.

The South Rim is the most accessible and a popular destination at Grand Canyon. The South Rim is where you'll find visitor's centers, historical buildings. It has over two dozen viewpoints and trailheads. Because of its popularity, visitors should expect crowds particularly in the busiest seasons, spring, summer, and fall. The North Rim has a shorter season, is harder to get to, is wilder, more secluded and more difficult.

Grandview Point offers an open scenic view of the canyon. This popular viewpoint offers panoramic views of Grand Canyon from east to west, including several bends of the Colorado River. This trail is incredibly steep. In summer, much of the trail is in full sun. In winter, ice and snow make hiking treacherous. Grandview Trail is a rocky trail that leads down into the depths of the Grand Canyon. The trail can be quite rugged, narrow, and steep,

Desert View drive has some scenic views of the Grand Canyon. You can take desert view drive to desert view road and visit the watchtower for some great scenic views. It is a very short walk to the watchtower. Less than a quarter mile walk. It was here that visitors to the canyon in the 1930's could sit in comfort and have outstanding views of the canyon.

Mather Point is a 5-minute walk from the South Rim visitor center, Mather Point is the first view the of Grand Canyon for many people. On a clear day you can see 30 miles to the east and 60 miles to the west. Thanks to its wide view and the dramatic rock formations, Mather Point is a popular place at Sunrise and Sunset. Be sure to get here early to enjoy the change in colors as the sun rises and sets.

Hopi Point offers panoramic and breathtaking views of the canyon along the scenic Hermit Road. Hopi Point offers five views of the Colorado River. An ideal location at sunrise or sunset. Hopi Point is accessible by the park's free shuttle bus service or a 2.5 mile walk along the Rim Trail. This wooden lookout tower is thought to be the first fire towers in Arizona.

Cape Royal Drive is a fantastic scenic road leading to various points. Including Walhalla Glades Pueblo, Point Imperial, and Cape Royal. Diverse viewpoints and several trails can be reached via this winding scenic drive that can be a great way to spend anywhere from a few hours to a day exploring the canyon.

Yaki Point is the only scenic viewpoint on Desert View Drive that is not accessible with a private vehicle. It can be reached using the free Kaibab Rim shuttle, from the Grand Canyon Visitor Center. The view of the canyon opens to the east, with the Desert View Watchtower visible in the distance. A popular view for sunset and sunrise, the lack of private vehicles provides a bit more solitude than other viewpoints.

The Navajo Bridge is the name of twin steel spandrel arch bridges that cross the Colorado River in the Grand Canyon National Park. Those traveling across the country on Highway 89A between Bitter Springs and Jacob Lake, AZ arrive at two bridges similar in appearance spanning the Colorado River. These two bridges, re one of only seven land crossings of the Colorado River for 750 miles.

East Rim Drive. This section is the only way to drive a car to many viewpoints. It has several viewpoints, where you can stop along the way. The drive is well worth the time for visitors who may not have one or two entire days to visit the Grand Canyon. If you are lucky, you will get to see elk and deer. Watch for elk grazing among the trees, especially south of the road.

Horseshoe bend, the Colorado River created a 1,000-foot deep, 270-degree horseshoe shaped bend in the Glen Canyon. The hike to the overlook is 1.5 miles round-trip over a hardened path. Horseshoe Bend is not part of the United States National Park System. Half of the U-shaped bend is owned by the city of Page, Arizona.

Lipan Point features some of the widest and most expansive canyon views along the South Rim, as well as the longest perspective of the Colorado River. This makes it an ideal spot to enjoy sunrise, sunset, and the night sky. On a clear day, you can see the Vermillion Cliffs 45 miles to the northeast and the curving river to the west as it enters the Inner Gorge of the canyon.

Mohave Point offers excellent views of the Colorado River deep in the canyon below. From here you can also see the Salt Creek, Granite, and Hermit rapids. Another spectacular point for watching the sunset. Mohave Point has a fine view of the near vertical, 3,000-foot-high cliffs. It's located off Hermit Road.

Cape Royal and Angel's Window are some of the only spots with views of the Colorado River from the North Rim. From the southeast side of the parking lot, a short wheelchair-accessible path leads to several spectacular viewpoints. The west side of the parking lot is where you can find a picnic area. Roundtrip hiking distance is 0.8 miles.

Powell Point is an overlook along the South Rim of the Grand Canyon. While a fine view of Grand Canyon is visible directly after stepping off the shuttle bus, a short, easy walk along the paved path out to the viewpoint is rewarded with even more excellent views and access to the Powell Memorial.

Toroweap point, also known as Tuweep Overlook a viewpoint of the Grand Canyon. It is in a remote area on the North Rim of the Grand Canyon. The Tuweep area of Grand Canyon National Park is remote and getting there is challenging. There is no water, gas, food, lodging, Wi-Fi, or cell service.

Pima Point is one of the best places on the rim to see, and sometimes hear, the Colorado River. The distant roar of Granite Rapids far below can be heard echoing up the canyon walls on quiet days. Located just before the end destination of West Rim Drive, Pima Point is a great place to stop and take a rest on the way to Hermit's Rest.

An unsigned dirt parking area marks the trail out to Shoshone Point. An easy one-mile walk along an old dirt road takes you through ponderosa forest, which eventually transitions to a juniper woodland near the rim of the canyon. A relatively quiet viewpoint along the rim of the canyon. Shoshone Point is the only area within the park that can be reserved for private events and gatherings.

Hermits Rest is a historic stop off Hermit Road, and the Canyon Rim Trail. It serves as the gateway to magnificent backcountry hiking trails that originate from the Hermit Trail, a steeply winding path into the canyon. Hermit trail offers a wide variety of hiking paths and experiences. This trail is for experienced desert hikers only.

One of the most awesome viewpoints of the Grand Canyon is at Guano Point. It has stunning 360-degree views of the canyon. Guano Point Cafe offers outside seating where you can sit and eat and enjoy the view of the canyon. The West Rim is where you'll find the world-famous Skywalk, Zipline, helicopter tours, scenic viewpoints, shopping and dining.

Grand Canyon Skywalk. Talk about a rush. Walk out on this U-Shaped glass bottom, see through floor structure that you can see awesome views of the Grand Canyon from. This will test your fear of heights. Skywalk gives you the feeling you are walking on air. Skywalk is located at Grand Canyon West's Eagle Point on the Hualapai Reservation and is not affiliated with Grand Canyon National Park. But we thought we would mention it. Because it would be fun to try, at least once.

Things to Do in the Grand Canyon

There's plenty of sightseeing opportunities in the Grand Canyon. But there's also some other fun things to do. Here's some of them.

Visitor Centers are both located on the North and South rim.

Visitor Center Theater. When the visitor center is open, the film, Grand Canyon, a Journey of Wonder, is shown. Admission is free.

Driving. The Canyon Rim Trail continues alongside Hermit Road, a 7-mile scenic road with 9 exceptional overlooks.

Walking, Hiking, Camping. walk part of the well-defined, and mostly level Canyon Rim Trail. Camping is available.

Activities for Kids. Grand Canyon's Junior Ranger program.

Bicycle. You can bring your own bike or rent one.

Guided Learning Adventures. Hiking, Mule Riding, Biking etc.

Mule Trips. 3-hour or overnight trips that travel the canyon rim.

Rafting Trips. Half-day and all-day smooth water trips

Grand Canyon Railway. Take a train ride, check for info.

Helicopter Rides. Take a Helicopter Tour Over the Canyon.

Check Before going. At certain times of the year some parts of the park are not open, and access may change. Reservations may be required.

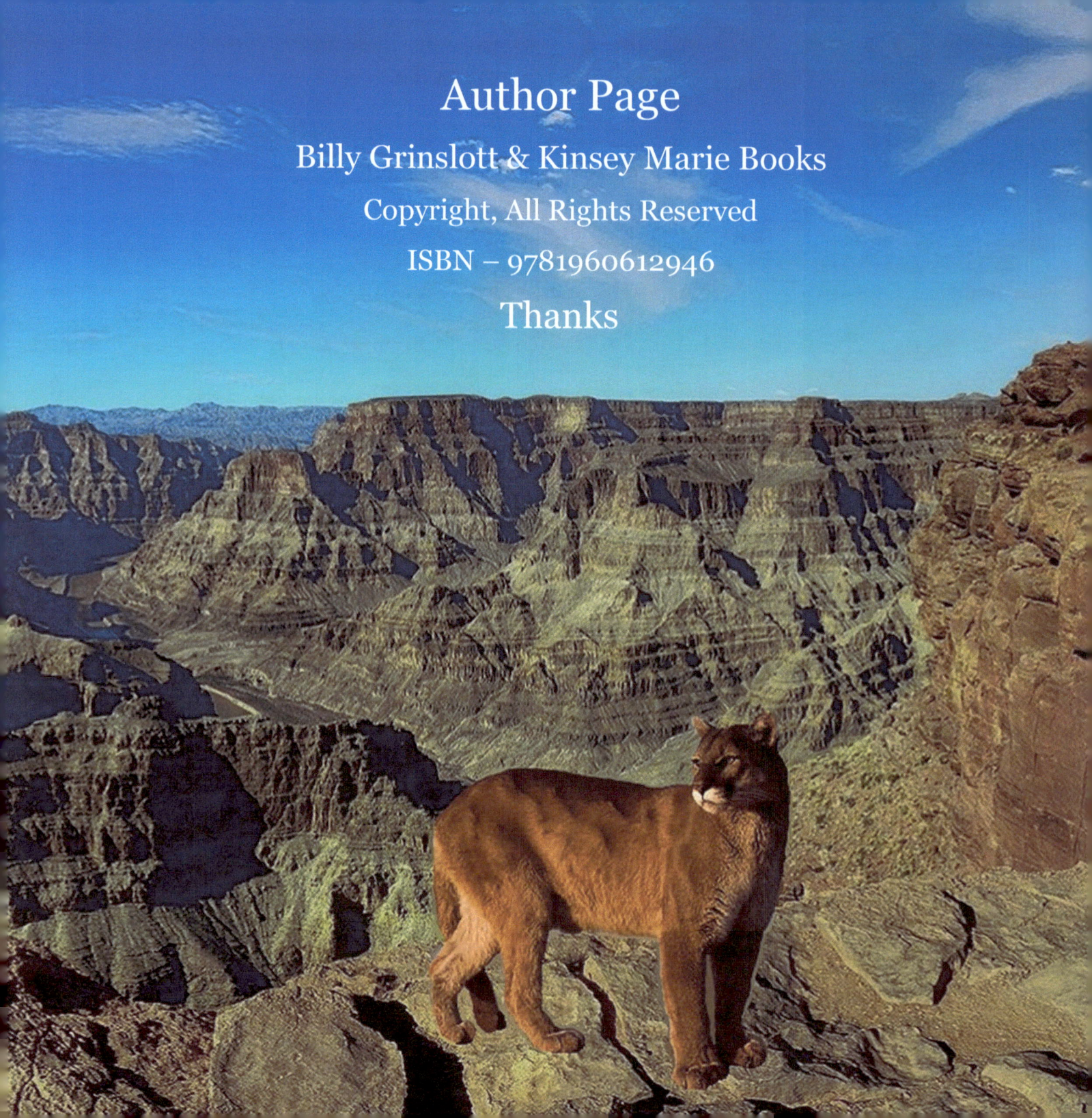

Author Page

Billy Grinslott & Kinsey Marie Books

Copyright, All Rights Reserved

ISBN – 9781960612946

Thanks

www.ingramcontent.com/pod-product-compliance
Lightning Source LLC
Chambersburg PA
CBHW060850270326

41934CB00002B/72